Centerville Library
Washington-Centerville Public Library
Centerville, Ohio

DISCARD

W9-CMC-265

FLOWER CROWNS
30 DIY FLORAL CREATIONS

FLOWER CROWNS
30 DIY FLORAL CREATIONS

CHRISTY MEISNER DORAMUS

Ulysses Press

Text copyright © 2015 Christy Meisner Doramus. Photos copyright © 2015 Luke Doramus. Design and concept copyright © 2015 Ulysses Press and its licensors. All rights reserved. Any unauthorized duplication in whole or in part or dissemination of this edition by any means (including but not limited to photocopying, electronic devices, digital versions, and the Internet) will be prosecuted to the fullest extent of the law.

Published in the U.S. by
Ulysses Press
P.O. Box 3440
Berkeley, CA 94703
www.ulyssespress.com

ISBN: 978-1-61243-447-6
Library of Congress Control Number 2014952005

Printed in Canada by Marquis Book Printing

10 9 8 7 6 5 4 3 2 1

Acquisitions editor: Katherine Furman
Project editor: Kelly Reed
Managing editor: Claire Chun
Editor: Renee Rutledge
Proofreader: Lauren Harrison
Front cover design: Michelle Thompson
Interior design: what!design @ whatweb.com
Layout and production: Jake Flaherty

Distributed by Publishers Group West

IMPORTANT NOTE TO READERS: This book is independently authored and published and no sponsorship or endorsement of this book by, and no affiliation with, any trademarked brands or other products mentioned within is claimed or suggested. All trademarks that appear in this book belong to their respective owners and are used here for informational purposes only. The author and publishers encourage readers to patronize the quality brands and products mentioned in this book.

To my family and friends – thank you all from the bottom of my heart for the support and encouragement.

CONTENTS

WINTER..............................93

SPECIAL OCCASIONS...................107

INTRODUCTION

Nothing compares to the feeling of wearing flowers in my hair. Whether it be an intricate flower crown or a simple wildflower tucked behind my ear, it imparts a feeling of instant joy.

In this book, I have shared some of my favorite floral hair accessory projects with you, using both fresh and faux flowers. From whimsical fresh flower crowns to easy faux flower hair clips, these DIY projects are fun to enjoy yourself or share with friends.

GETTING STARTED

SEASONALITY

Before searching for fresh flowers to make your crown, it is important to understand what is in season at the time. Most of the projects in this book are made with blooms that are generally easy to find, but do keep seasonality in mind when planning your designs. Peonies, for instance, can be elusive in September.

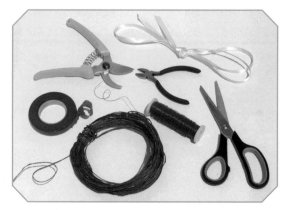

SUPPLIES

Most of the projects in this book require the same set of tools: florist wire, moss-covered wire, scissors or garden shears, and ribbon.

FLORIST WIRE

Many varieties of florist wire are suggested in this book. I use both precut wire sticks and wire on a roll. When selecting your own florist wire, make sure that it is not so thick that it is difficult to maneuver or bend. When making faux flower projects, I generally choose a thicker wire than that used for making fresh flower pieces.

HOW TO WEAR YOUR FLOWER CROWN

Throughout this book, I show you how to secure your flower crown to ribbon, which is generally the easiest option when making something that you want to adjust in the back or wear with different hairstyles. The ribbon can be tied underneath your hair, on top of the hair, or even woven into a braid.

FLOWER GLOSSARY

When making fresh flower crowns, I constantly find myself turning to these 12 select blooms—my favorites.

WAX FLOWERS

I love wax flowers because they really mix well with other blooms, big or small. They come in different colors depending on the season and add volume and texture to a flower crown. Added bonus—they smell minty fresh and hold their shape well.

FREESIA

Freesia blooms in white or lavender smell amazing and are a great addition to a flower crown. Also, freesia greenery woven into a crown attains a very whimsical look.

SPRAY ROSES

For a lush, romantic flower crown, I love using spray roses for their fullness and range of colors. Standard roses are generally too big to hold up in a crown, but spray roses are smaller and much easier to maneuver.

ROSEMARY

I love using rosemary at the base of my flower crowns, especially in the fall and winter. The smell is incredible and it dries quite nicely.

DRIED LAVENDER

Who doesn't love lavender's scent, color, and shape? It is an amazing option for a great-smelling or long-lasting crown.

GLOBE AMARANTH

This funky flower is one of my favorites due to its fuzzy texture and round shape. It comes in several colors and looks playful and unique when incorporated into a crown with other flowers. It also keeps its shape for weeks, which makes it a good option for a long-lasting crown.

SEEDED EUCALYPTUS

The texture of seeded eucalyptus has so much personality! It can look organic when woven into a crown with other greenery, but also adds a funky and free-spirited element to traditional blooms.

RANUNCULUS

Like spray roses, ranunculus come in many colors and look incredibly lush and full in a flower crown. You can't go wrong when incorporating these statement blooms into any crown or flower arrangement.

BABY'S BREATH

This "filler flower" has a reputation of its own, but it looks incredibly sweet in a flower crown. Use it alone for a flower girl's crown or mixed in with colorful flowers for a fuller look. It's also always in season and very easy to find.

DELPHINIUMS

If you are looking to incorporate bright blues or purples into your flower crown, I would suggest turning to delphiniums. These gorgeous blooms may not always be the easiest to find, but they make a colorful statement.

ASTILBE

This pretty pink variety is not always the easiest to find, but I always turn to it when adding pink elements to my flower crowns. Solidago is also a great alternative if you prefer bright yellows with the same texture.

AGERATUM

I am always on the hunt for good filler flowers to add volume to my flower crowns. This one has it all—color, texture, and shape!

SPRING

Whether you are headed to Coachella or enjoying the year's first stint of warm weather, these cheerful floral crowns and hair accessories are the perfect way to bring out your inner flower child.

FRESH DAISY FLOWER CROWN

The daisy crown is probably the most iconic for music festivals and poolside gatherings. There is something so happy about a daisy, and this crown brings instant cheer. This style can be created very affordably with a bundle of daisies from your local grocery store or flower market. If you are lucky enough to grow them in your own backyard, even better!

WHAT YOU WILL NEED

9 daisies in a color of your choice

6–8 feet of florist wire

scissors or garden shears

2 yards of ribbon

1: Clip the stems of all 9 daisies about ¼ inch away from the bloom. Also cut 9 pieces of florist wire, about 4 inches each.

2: Feed 1 piece of wire through the stem and center of each bloom and create a small hook at one end.

3: Pull the hook very gently into the center of the bloom to secure.

4: Repeat steps 2–4 until all 9 daisies are secured to wire stems.

5: Begin forming your crown with 1 daisy, bending its new wire stem gently to the right. Place a second daisy about 1½–2 inches away from the first bloom and bend its wire stem to the right, twisting it together with the wire stem from the first.

6: Continue adding the daisies to the growing chain one by one, twisting the wire stem together and to the right with each bloom added. The florist wire base will allow you to bend the entire strand into a half moon shape.

TIP: If you would like the daisies to go all the way around your head, continue adding blooms until you reach the desired flower crown size.

7: Once the last daisy has been added, bend the end of the wire to prevent it from scratching or catching.

TIP: If you bend the wire into a loop, this will also give you a great place to tie the ribbon.

8: Cut the ribbon into two 1-yard pieces, one for each side of the finished flower crown. Fold each 1-yard piece in half, creating a loop and securing the ribbon to the gathered stems with a loop knot. After pulling this knot tightly, use the two ends to tie a second knot to secure. Repeat on other side.

TIP: You can cover the florist wire by wrapping it with florist tape to make the base of this crown more comfortable to wear all day.

MARDI GRAS FAUX FLOWER CROWN

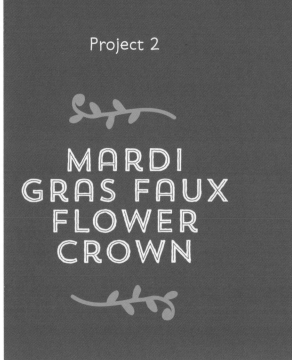

Celebrate carnival season with this faux flower crown that will last throughout your week-long festivities. The faux blooms used to create this crown consist of small and large golden roses, green hydrangea blooms, and purple delphinium flowers.

WHAT YOU WILL NEED

medium to large purple, green, and gold faux blooms

6–8 feet of florist wire

a 20- to 24-inch strand of moss-covered wire

florist tape

scissors

2 yards of ribbon

1: Begin creating pliable wire stems for each of your faux blooms. Thread a 4- to 6-inch piece of florist wire through the center of the faux yellow rose and create a hook on one end.

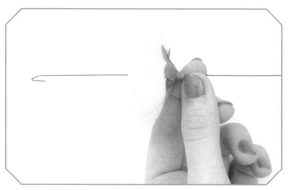

TIP: When shopping for faux flowers, those that have holes through the center of the bloom are easiest to secure into a crown.

2: Pull the hook into the center of the yellow rose bloom to secure.

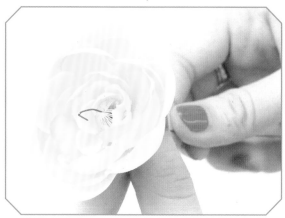

3: Begin to create a faux stem for the second flower by threading a piece of 4- to 6-inch florist wire through the center of the purple delphinium bloom, pulling the flower to the middle of the piece of wire.

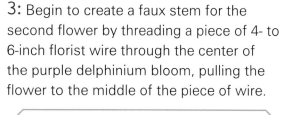

4: Bring the ends of the florist wire together, creating a V shape and leaving the flower in the center.

5: Tightly twist the two ends of florist wire together starting at the base of the flower, creating a pliable wire stem for the flower.

6: Thread a 4- to 6-inch piece of florist wire through the green hydrangea bloom, leaving it in the center.

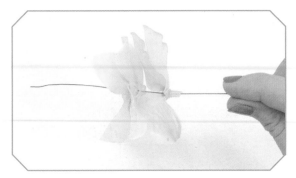

7: Repeat steps 4 and 5.

8: Once you create wire stems for each bloom you plan to use, lay them out to begin making the flower crown. This crown can include anywhere from 12–20 blooms depending on how long or full you want the finished product to be.

9: Begin forming the crown by placing the base of the first bloom approximately 2 inches away from the end of the moss-covered wire strand.

10: Twist the wire stem around the moss-covered wire strand multiple times, moving in a spiral toward the right to secure the bloom to the strand.

11: Add the second bloom and repeat step 10.

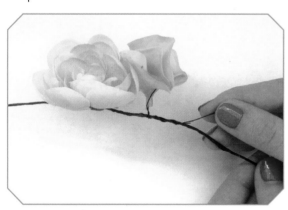

12: Add the third bloom and repeat step 10.

13: Continue adding blooms to the growing strand while creating a flower and color pattern of your choice.

14: Once you have reached the desired length for your crown, create a loop with the end of the moss-covered wire.

15: Wrap the end of the moss-covered wire in a spiral beginning at the base of the loop and moving backward toward the flowers, covering any loose wire. This step helps you to achieve a cleaner look at the ends of your crown and also creates a loop for threading ribbon.

16: Begin wrapping the base of the crown with florist tape to cover any sharp wires. This step is not required to complete the crown, but gives it a cleaner look and makes it more comfortable to wear.

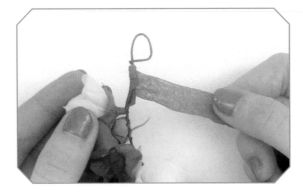

17: Continue wrapping the base of the flower crown with florist wire until the bottom looks like this.

18: Cut two 1-yard pieces of ribbon. Fold a piece in half and feed it through a loop, pulling through to create a loop knot. Repeat on the other side. The ribbons will allow you to adjust the crown to fit on your head.

Project 3

PRETTY PASTELS FRESH FLOWER CROWN

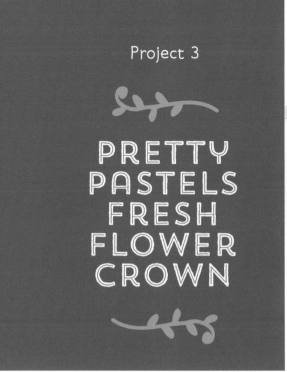

Perfect for springtime and Easter celebrations, this pastel fresh floral crown is a cheerful accessory that looks amazing when paired with a sweet lightweight dress. The flowers used to create this crown include purple delphiniums, light blue tweedia flowers, and pink tulips.

WHAT YOU WILL NEED

a variety of 3–5 fresh flower types in pastel shades

4–6 feet of florist wire

a 20- to 24-inch strand of moss-covered wire

scissors or garden shears

2 yards of ribbon

1: Gather 1–3 small sprigs of the first pastel bloom (blue), cutting the stems no longer than 3–4 inches long. Pinch the bunch together with your thumb and index finger, holding it 3–4 inches away from the end of the moss-covered wire. Secure everything together with florist wire.

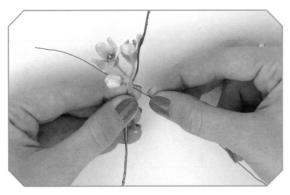

2: Begin adding in the second pastel flower (purple), covering the wire-wrapped bunch with the bloom.

3: Wrap the second bloom to the growing flower chain by wrapping it around the moss-covered wire with florist wire, moving in a spiral motion downward.

4: Add your third pastel bloom (pink) to the growing floral chain.

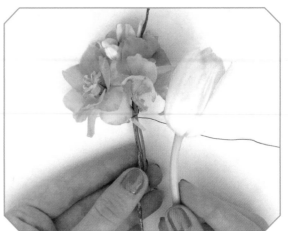

5: Continue twisting the pastel flowers to the bundle one to two at a time in the pattern of your choice, wrapping each to the growing chain with florist wire in a spiral motion downward.

6: Once you have reached the end of your florist wire piece, bend it to secure and add another piece before securing additional flowers.

7: Once you have reached the desired length of your flower crown, pull the two ends together to create a circular shape.

8: Take the end of the moss-covered wire strand and create a loop, preparing to twist the leftover piece around itself.

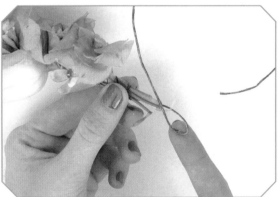

9: Once the moss-covered wire is completely twisted around itself, create the same loop on the other side of the crown.

10: Cut the ribbon into two 1-yard pieces, one for each side of the finished pastel fresh flower crown. Fold each 1-yard piece in half, creating a loop.

11: Feed the folded ribbon through the moss-covered wire loops.

12: Secure the ribbon to the loops on either side of the crown with a loop knot to finish.

Project 4

PRECIOUS PEONY FAUX FLOWER CROWN

Peony season need never end with this faux statement crown.

WHAT YOU WILL NEED

5–7 faux peonies

scissors

a 20- to 24-inch strand of moss-covered wire

6–10 feet of florist wire

florist tape

2 yards of ribbon

1: Separate the peony blooms from their original stems.

2: Begin creating a wire stem for your first peony bloom by pulling back a couple of the petals. Then, place a 6- to 10-inch piece of florist wire where the petals meet the base of the bloom, hiding it inside of the peony. Make sure that the center of the wire is placed underneath the petals, as you will need the two ends of the wire to be at least 2–3 inches each.

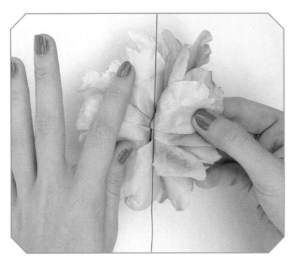

3: Pull the ends of the wire behind the base of the peony flower.

4: Bring the two wire ends together and cross them tightly at the back of the bloom.

5: Twist the two strands of wire together tightly to create the wire stem. If the peony does not feel secure on its new stem, repeat steps 2–3 on the opposite side of the bloom, placing a second piece of wire under two different petals.

6: Repeat steps 2–5 until each peony is prepared on a new wire stem.

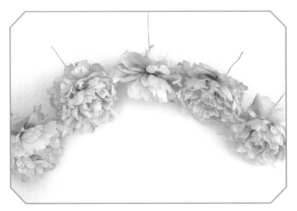

7: Begin forming the crown by placing the base of the first peony approximately 2–3 inches away from the end of the moss-covered wire strand.

8: Secure the bloom to the moss-covered wire by bending the flower's wire stem up and to the right, proceeding to wrap it around in a spiral motion moving from left to right.

9: Add a second peony and repeat step 8.

10: As you continue adding each peony, the base of your crown should look like this.

11: Once you have added in all of the blooms and are ready to finish the ends of your crown, create a loop with the end of the moss-covered wire.

12: Wrap the excess moss-covered wire around itself beginning at the base of the loop and moving backward toward the flowers, covering any loose wire. Repeat on opposite side.

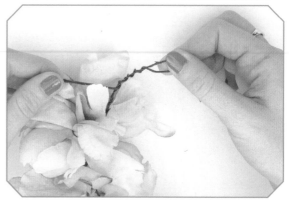

13: Wrap the base of the flower crown with florist tape to cover up any sharp wire ends, ultimately making the finished crown more comfortable to wear.

14: As you wrap the base of the crown with florist tape, pull it tight and move in a spiral motion from left to right to make sure it looks as clean as possible. The tape is self-adhesive, so although it will feel tacky, it sticks to itself for easy application.

15: Once the base of your crown is completely covered in florist tape, it should look like this.

16: Cut 2 pieces of ribbon, 1 yard each. Fold each piece in half and feed it through the loop, pulling through to create a secure knot on both sides.

FAUX FLOWER HEADBAND

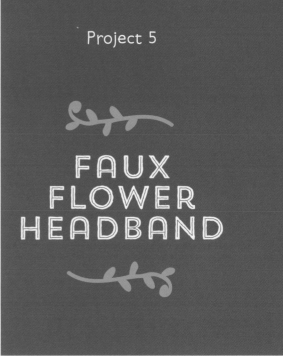

A great alternative to a traditional flower crown, this faux flower headband is an elegant accessory that's easy to wear.

WHAT YOU WILL NEED

5–7 faux flowers (ranunculus shown here)

scissors

1–2 feet of florist tape

2–3 feet of florist wire

a headband that matches your hair color

1: Clip the stems off of each faux flower and cut a 4- to 6-inch piece of florist wire for each one.

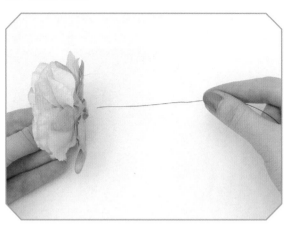

2: Begin creating a pliable wire stem for your first faux bloom by threading a 4- to 6-inch piece of florist wire through the center.

3: Fold the piece of florist wire in half, pulling the end toward the base of the bloom.

4: Bring the two ends of the florist wire together.

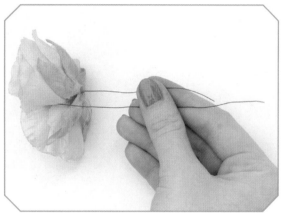

5: Twist the two strands of florist wire tightly together, ultimately creating a wire stem for the bloom.

6: Repeat steps 2–5 for each flower until they are all on wire stems.

7: Place the base of the first flower against the top and center of the headband.

8: Begin securing the flower to your headpiece by twisting the wire stem around the headband from left to right.

9: Place a second flower next to the first and repeat step 8.

10: Continue placing each flower on the headband, securing it with the wire stem.

11: The inside of your headband should look like this once all of the flowers are attached.

12: To conceal the messy florist wire and prevent it from pulling the hair, cover the base of the headband with florist tape by wrapping it around the section where the flowers have been placed.

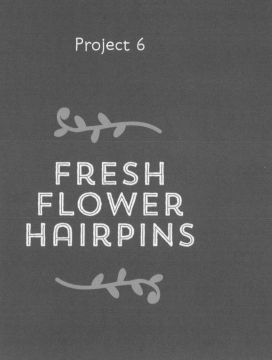

FRESH FLOWER HAIRPINS

Replace your jewelry with these fresh flower hairpins to add an instant boho vibe to any hairstyle.

WHAT YOU WILL NEED

fresh blooms (small to medium flowers such as these purple scabiosa flowers work well)

bobby pins

scissors or garden shears

3–5 inches of florist wire and 3–5 inches of florist tape per hairpin

1: Clip the stem of the bloom, leaving approximately 2 inches from the base of the flower. Prepare to secure the flower to the bobby pin by cutting a 3- to 5-inch piece of florist wire.

2: Place the flower's stem against the wavy side of the bobby pin and hold in place.

3: Thread the florist wire through the loop of the bobby pin, using it to secure the flower to the wavy side by wrapping the two together from top to bottom.

TIP: The flower will stay in place better if secured to the wavy side of the bobby pin because it allows the florist wire to hold on without slipping as it may on the straight side.

4: Your bobby pin should now look like this. Make sure not to wrap the bobby pin shut, but only secure the flower to one side, allowing it to open fully.

5: Cut a 3- to 5-inch piece of florist tape and prepare to use it to cover the wire-wrapped side of the bobby pin.

6: Completely wrap the wavy side of the bobby pin, including the end, with the tacky florist tape, which will stick to itself. This step will prevent the wire from pulling or scratching when placed in the hair.

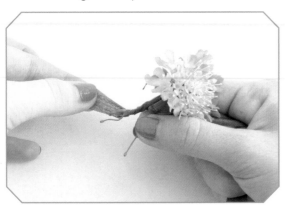

7: Cut off the excess florist tape.

8: Pin the finished product into your hair as you would a regular bobby pin.

SUMMER

Complete your midsummer outfit with these fresh and faux floral hair accessories that can be worn anywhere from the beach to a barbecue. With so many amazing fresh blooms available during this season, your options are limitless.

STATEMENT BLOOM FRESH FLOWER CROWN

This bright and cheery floral crown is made with a statement bloom and designed to wear on one side of the head for a pop of playful color.

WHAT YOU WILL NEED

greenery such as seeded eucalyptus or rosemary

small neutral flowers such as the ranunculus used here

a bold statement bloom like this bright yellow tree peony

scissors or garden shears

a 20- to 24-inch strand of moss-covered wire

4–6 feet of florist wire

1: Create the base of your flower crown using a piece of fresh rosemary approximately 3–4 inches long and wrapping it to the moss-covered wire strand with florist wire, moving in a spiral motion from left to right.

2: Add 1–2 more sprigs of greenery to the bundle and wrap everything together from left to right with florist wire to create a growing chain.

3: Once you have added approximately 6–10 inches of greenery, begin adding your neutral blooms (2–3) to the floral chain.

4: Wrap 2–3 of the smaller, neutral blooms to the bundle with florist wire, continuing to move in a spiral motion from left to right.

5: Prepare your statement bloom by creating a wire stem. Begin this process by clipping the bloom from its original stem, then threading a 6- to 8-inch piece of florist wire through the center of the bloom.

6: Fold the piece of florist wire in half, pulling the end toward the base of the bloom.

7: Gently pull the flower petals apart as you pull the florist wire through them to the other side of the bloom.

8: Bring the two ends of the florist wire together.

9: Repeat steps 5–8, moving the wire through the petals on the opposite side of the flower for increased security, and twist all the wires together behind the bloom to complete the wire stem.

10: Add your statement flower to the flower chain. Place the base of the bloom next to the smaller, neutral flowers and secure it to the bundle by wrapping it to the chain with its wire stem as you continue to move from left to right.

11: On the opposite side of the statement bloom, repeat the pattern with the smaller, neutral flowers, securing them to the chain with florist wire.

12: Finish the other end of the flower chain by adding a final piece of rosemary equal in size to the one you used in step 1.

13: Use florist wire to wrap the rosemary around the moss-covered wire, moving in a spiral motion toward the end.

14: Secure the end of the chain by wrapping the end of the moss-covered wire around the piece of rosemary a couple of times.

15: Pull the two ends of moss-covered wire together to form a circle.

16: Twist the moss-covered wire ends together to complete the flower crown.

FOURTH OF JULY FRESH FLOWER CROWN

Show off your patriotic spirit at the beach or barbecue with this fresh red, white, and blue flower crown. To create this crown, you will use blue hydrangeas, red ranunculus, and white wax flowers.

WHAT YOU WILL NEED

assorted red, white, and blue flowers

6–8 feet of florist wire

scissors or garden shears

2 yards of ribbon

1: Clip small sections of the blue hydrangeas and white wax flowers approximately 3 inches from the base of the blooms. Also, clip the stem of the red ranunculus close to the base of the flower, leaving about ¼ inch of stem.

TIP: Spray roses are also a great substitute for this look if you are not able to find ranunculus.

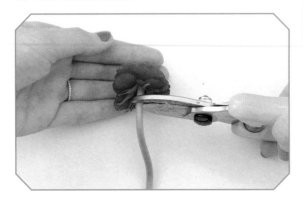

2: Cut a 4-inch piece of florist wire and feed it through the red ranunculus stem and bloom.

3: Create a small hook with the end of the florist wire and pull it carefully into the ranunculus bloom to secure.

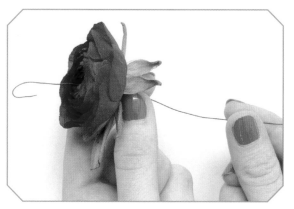

TIP: Pulling the hooked florist wire through the bloom ensures that the bloom will face outward in the final crown.

4: Gather 3–5 sprigs of the white wax flowers. Wrap a new 10- to 12-inch piece of florist wire around the bunch in a spiral motion from left to right, securing the stems to the piece of wire that is holding the red ranunculus.

5: Gather 3–5 sprigs of the blue hydrangeas and place them into the red and white bunch, wrapping the wire around the group of stems to create a growing strand of flowers.

6: Repeat steps 1–3 and add another red ranunculus, twisting the florist wire from the base of the stem around the growing strand of flowers from left to right.

7: Continue adding small bunches of blue hydrangeas and white wax flowers, alternating with the red ranunculus blooms. Wrap each piece into the growing strand of flowers.

8: Once you have reached the desired flower crown length, clip the group of stems so they are all the same length, at least ½ inch away from the wire that holds them all together. Create a loop with the end of the moss- covered wire and wrap the end of the strand in a spiral beginning at the base of the loop moving backward toward the flowers to cover any loose florist wire. Repeat on the other side.

9: Cut 2 pieces of ribbon, 1 yard each. Fold each piece in half and feed one through each of the two loops you just created. Pull the loop tightly, then use the two ends to tie a second knot to secure.

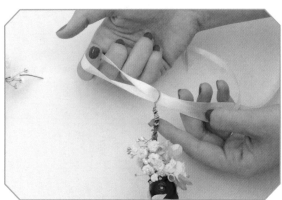

Project 9

FAUX FLOWER SUMMER VACATION CROWN

This small faux flower crown can be packed away in a suitcase for an easy boho outfit update, no matter where you may land. Various rosebuds, ranunculus, and daisies were used to create this white and yellow crown.

WHAT YOU WILL NEED

assorted small to medium faux blooms in colors of your choice

6–8 feet of florist wire

a 20- to 24-inch strand of moss-covered wire

scissors

2 yards of ribbon

florist tape

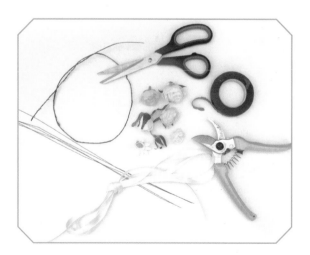

1: Clip the stems off of each of your faux flowers. Begin creating a pliable wire stem for your first faux bloom by threading a 4- to 6-inch piece of florist wire through the center of the small faux white rose and create a hook on one end.

3: Bring the two ends of florist wire together at the base of the original rose stem and pull tightly from the center of the flower, allowing the wire to hold the bloom together where the base of the petals meet the stem.

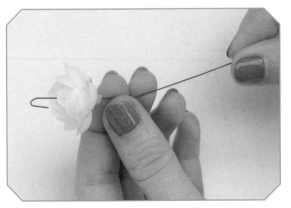

2: Create a pliable wire stem for the second rosebud by pulling two of the petals back and placing the center of an 8- to 10-inch piece of florist wire against the base of the flower petal.

4: Twist the two ends of the florist wire together tightly, creating a faux stem that holds the bloom in place.

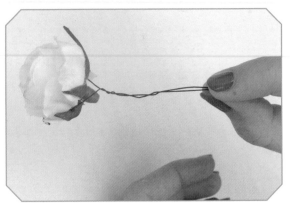

5: When creating a wire stem for the daisy, place an 8- to 10-inch piece of florist wire behind the center of the flower, being careful not to separate the stem from the flower.

6: Repeat steps 3 and 4 to complete the wire stem on the daisy.

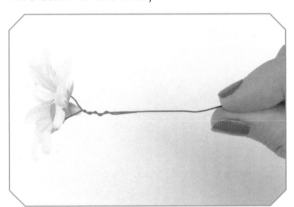

7: For this tight rosebud, repeat step 2, but instead of pulling back the petals, do the same underneath the attached greenery.

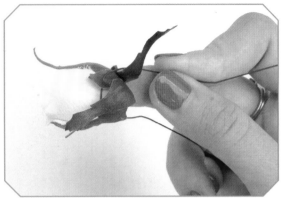

8: Repeat steps 3 and 4 to complete the stem for the tight rosebud. Continue creating pliable wire stems for all of your blooms.

9: Once you create wire stems for each bloom you plan to use, lay them out and prepare to make the flower crown. This crown can have anywhere from 20–40 blooms depending on how long or full you want the finished product to be.

10: Begin forming the crown by placing the base of the first white bloom approximately 2 inches away from the end of the moss-covered wire strand.

11: Secure the bloom to the moss-covered wire by bending the flower's wire stem up and to the right and proceeding to wrap it around in a spiral motion moving from left to right.

12: Add the second bloom, repeating steps 10 and 11.

13: Add the third bloom, repeating steps 10 and 11.

14: Continue repeating steps 10 and 11 until you have reached the desired crown length. The bottom of the crown should look like this.

15: Once you are ready to finish the ends of your crown, create a loop with the end of the moss-covered wire and wrap the excess from the base of the loop toward the flowers, covering any loose wire.

16: Repeat step 15 on the opposite side. Your crown should look like this once both loops have been created.

17: Wrap the base of the flower crown with florist tape to cover up any sharp wires, ultimately making the finished crown more comfortable to wear.

18: Cut 2 pieces of ribbon, 1 yard each. Fold each piece in half and feed one through each loop, pulling through to create a knot to finish each end.

Project 10

MIDSUMMER FRESH FLOWER CROWN

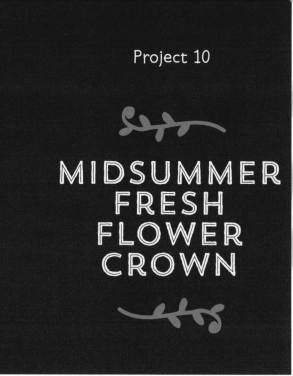

This whimsical flower crown is made of simple and affordable summer blooms that can easily be found at your local deli or grocery store. The yellow, white, and purple flowers come together to form a delicate and neutral crown that will look amazing paired with any summer frock. Flowers used to create this crown include Queen Anne's lace, purple limonium, solidago, and white aster.

WHAT YOU WILL NEED

3–5 assorted flowers of your choice

4–6 feet of florist wire

scissors or garden shears

2 yards of ribbon

1: Begin by gathering 3–5 sprigs of the assorted blooms (3–4 inches each) and pinching them together with your thumb and index finger.

2: Cut a piece of florist wire approximately 10–12 inches and twist it around the gathered stems two to three times to secure.

3: Gather 3–5 additional sprigs of assorted flowers and pinch them together along with the secured bundle.

4: Using florist wire, continue twisting small bundles of flowers into the growing strand.

5: Repeat steps 3 and 4, adding blooms in the order of your choice.

6: Once your original strand of florist wire has been completely twisted around the bunch, cut another 10- to 12-inch piece of wire and continue pinching the small sprigs together and wrapping them into the growing strand.

TIP: Longer pieces of wire may be more difficult to maneuver, so it is best to use 3–4 pieces to make your flower crown versus trying to use one continuous piece.

7: Once you have achieved the desired flower crown length, secure each end of the strand by twisting florist wire around the last bundle of blooms. Then, fold 1 yard of ribbon in half and tie a loop knot around the end of the crown, leaving at least ½ inch of stems from the edge.

8: Once the ribbon is secured to the bundle, gather each end of the ribbon and tie them together into a second and final knot for security. Repeat on the opposite side.

SUMMER CONCERT FRESH FLOWER CROWN

This delicate and bohemian flower crown is a great summer music festival accessory and looks particularly amazing paired with a lightweight dress or jeans. Pictured from left to right here, the flowers used to create this crown include white wax flowers, white and purple wildflowers, chamomile flowers, and assorted greenery.

WHAT YOU WILL NEED

a variety of 3–5 small flowers

4–6 feet of florist wire

20–24 inches of moss-covered wire
scissors or garden shears

2 yards of ribbon

1: Gather 2–4 small sprigs of assorted flowers, cutting and leaving each stem no longer than 3–4 inches. Pinch the bunch and the moss-covered wire together with your thumb and index finger. Hold this bunch together while preparing to form a flower chain.

2: Use a 10- to 12-inch piece of florist wire to secure the first bunch to the moss-covered wire by wrapping the two together, moving in a spiral motion two to three times around. Clip another group of 3–5 flowers to add in.

3: Continue adding small bunches of flowers to the growing chain and securing them with florist wire, wrapping each new bunch one to three times before adding another. Create a pattern of your choice as you add each new bunch of flowers.

5: Once you have reached the desired crown length, cut the stems at the ends of the crown to the same length (about 1 inch away from the last piece of wrapped florist wire). Then, create a loop with the excess moss-covered wire, which will be used to cover the ends of the crown, hiding the stems and florist wire.

4: When you reach the desired crown length, because the flowers are secured to the moss-covered wire base, the entire chain will bend very easily, yet still remain sturdy.

6: Wrap the moss-covered wire from the base of the loop and around the cut stems for additional security on each end of the crown.

7: Cut 2 pieces of ribbon, 1 yard each. Fold each piece in half and feed one through each loop you just created, pulling through to create a knot on both sides. The ribbons will allow you to adjust the crown to fit on your head, no matter what hairstyle you choose.

FRESH SUNFLOWER CROWN

This bold sunflower crown is the perfect accessory for occasions spent savoring the last days of summer.

WHAT YOU WILL NEED

7–9 sunflowers (smaller varieties work best)

6–10 feet of florist wire

scissors or garden shears

2 feet of ribbon

a 20- to 24-inch strand of moss-covered wire

1: Clip the stems of each sunflower about ½ inch away from the bloom and cut one piece of florist wire for each flower, approximately 6 inches each.

2: Feed one piece of florist wire through the stem and center of each bloom, creating a large hook with one end of the wire.

3: Feed the florist wire hook through the center of the sunflower.

4: Pull the wire all the way through the stem and bring the two ends of wire together.

5: Twist the two ends of florist wire tightly together behind the bloom to create a wire stem that supports the sunflower.

6: Repeat steps 2–5 until all sunflowers are secured to florist wire stems.

7: Begin building your crown by placing one sunflower stem against the moss-covered wire, approximately 4 inches from the end. Bend the base of the wire stem up toward the right.

8: Twist the wire stem completely around the moss-covered wire, moving from left to right.

9: Continue adding the sunflowers one by one, twisting the wire stems together and to the right, repeating steps 7 and 8 for each new bloom.

10: Once you have added all of the sunflowers to the moss-covered wire, bend it into a half-moon shape to form the crown.

11: Take the end of the moss-covered wire and create a loop at the end of the strand, preparing to twist the leftover piece around itself.

12: Once the moss-covered wire is completely twisted around itself, each side of the crown should have a loop that looks like this.

13: Cut the ribbon into two 1-yard pieces, one for each side of the finished sunflower crown. Fold each 1-yard piece in half, creating a loop.

14: Feed the folded ribbon through the moss-covered wire loops and secure with loop knots on both ends.

AUTUMN

Floral hair accessories are no longer just for the spring and summer. As the leaves begin to change color, embrace harvest season with these flower crowns and hairpieces designed to accessorize all of your fall ensembles, from a gameday outfit to a Halloween costume.

FALL HARVEST FRESH FLOWER CROWN

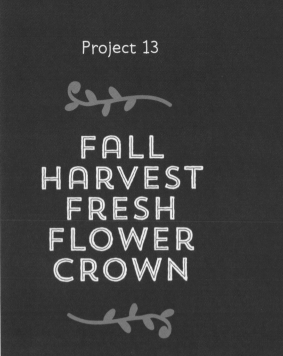

Celebrate harvest season with this textured, autumn-inspired fresh flower crown made with leaves, seeded eucalyptus, rosemary, dried lavender, and light pink globe amaranth.

WHAT YOU WILL NEED

a variety of 4–6 seasonal fall blooms or leaves

6–10 feet of florist wire

a 20- to 24-inch strand of moss-covered wire

scissors or garden shears

2 yards of ribbon

1: Create the base of your flower crown by cutting a piece of fresh rosemary approximately 3–4 inches long and securing it to the moss-covered wire strand with a 3- to 5-inch piece of florist wire, wrapping it in a spiral motion from left to right.

2: Pinch 2–3 other flowers or leaves together and prepare to wrap them together with the rosemary and moss-covered wire using a new 10- to 12-inch piece of florist wire.

TIP: When using rosemary, choose the tips of the plant over the thick stems, as they are generally the most pliable and work best for bending pieces into the crown. It will also keep your crown smelling amazing for days.

3: Continue to build the crown by adding small groups of flowers into the growing strand, wrapping them together with florist wire in a spiral motion from left to right.

TIP: It is generally best to add no more than 3–4 sprigs at a time to keep the crown intact and prevent pieces from falling out.

4: Add a second piece of rosemary to continue building the fullness of the crown, wrapping it to the growing strand with florist wire.

5: Repeat steps 3 and 4 until you have reached the desired crown length and design.

6: Once you have reached the desired crown length, take the end of the moss-covered florist wire and create a loop at the end of the strand.

7: Wrap the end of the moss-covered wire in a spiral beginning at the base of the loop and moving backward toward the flowers to cover any loose wire.

8: Cut 2 pieces of ribbon, 1 yard each. Fold each piece in half and feed one through each loop, pulling through to create a knot. The ribbons will allow you to adjust the crown to fit on your head, no matter what hairstyle you choose.

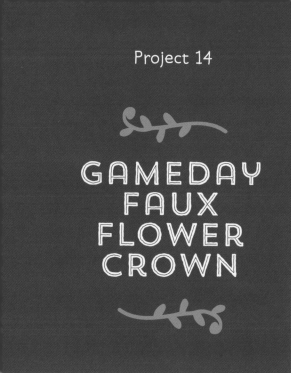

GAMEDAY FAUX FLOWER CROWN

Show your spirit on gameday with a faux flower crown in your team's colors. This design can be customized using faux flowers in any color, size, or shape. For this crown, white rose, orange ranunculus, and blue delphinium are used.

WHAT YOU WILL NEED

assorted medium-large faux blooms in the team colors of your choice

8–10 feet of florist wire

a 20- to 24-inch strand of moss-covered wire

scissors or garden shears

2 yards of ribbon

florist tape

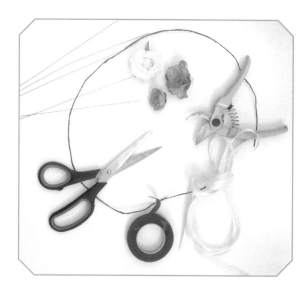

1: Begin by separating the faux blooms from their stems and creating pliable wire stems for each of them. Thread a 4- to 6-inch piece of florist wire through the center of the faux orange bloom and create a hook on one end.

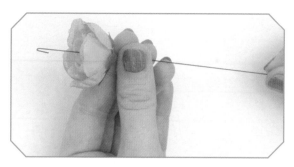

2: Pull the hook into the center of the orange bloom to secure.

3: Create a pliable wire stem for the white rose by pulling two of the petals back and placing the center of a 12- to 14-inch piece of florist wire against the base of the flower.

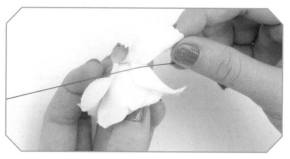

4: Bring the two ends of florist wire together at the base of the original rose stem and pull tightly from the center of the flower, allowing the wire to hold the bloom together where the base of the petals meet the stem.

5: Twist the two ends of the florist wire together tightly, creating a faux stem that holds the bloom in place.

6: Create a stem for the blue delphinium bloom by threading a piece of 4- to 6-inch florist wire through the center and pulling the flower to the middle of the piece of wire.

7: Bring the ends of the florist wire together, creating a V shape and leaving the flower in the center.

8: Repeat step 5 for the blue delphinium bloom.

9: Once you create wire stems for each bloom you plan to use, lay them out and prepare to begin making the flower crown. This crown can have anywhere from 12–20 blooms depending on how long or full you want the finished product to be.

10: Begin forming the crown by placing the base of the first orange bloom approximately 2 inches away from the end of the moss-covered wire strand.

11: Secure the bloom to the moss-covered wire by wrapping the flower's wire stem around it in a spiral motion moving to the right.

12: Add the second bloom and repeat step 11.

13: Add the third bloom and repeat step 11.

14: The bottom of your crown will begin to look like this.

15: Continue adding blooms until you have reached the desired crown size.

16: Create a loop with the end of the moss-covered wire and wrap the excess, beginning at the base of the loop and moving backward toward the flowers to cover any loose wire.

17: Wrap the base of the flower crown with florist tape to cover up any sharp wires, ultimately making the finished crown more comfortable to wear.

18: Your wrapped crown will look like this at the bottom.

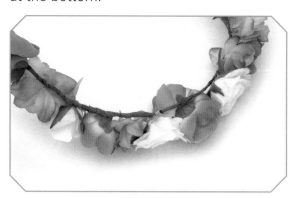

19: Once the loops are created on either side of the crown and the base is wrapped with florist tape, you are ready to add ribbon, which helps to adjust the size of the crown on your head.

20: Cut 2 pieces of ribbon, 1 yard each. Fold each piece in half and feed one through each loop, pulling through with a loop knot to finish.

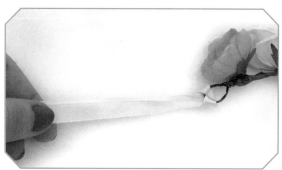

PUMPKIN PATCH FRESH FLOWER CROWN

This fresh flower crown is perfect for Halloween season and a great way to embrace the cooler temperatures without completely letting go of sunnier days. The flowers used to create this crown include orange spray roses, greenery, and white globe amaranth.

WHAT YOU WILL NEED

a variety of 3–5 small flowers, one being a statement orange shade, such as spray roses

4–6 feet of florist wire

a 20- to 24-inch strand of moss-covered wire

scissors or garden shears

2 yards of ribbon

1: Gather 2–4 small sprigs of assorted flowers, cutting and leaving the stems no longer than 3–4 inches long. Along with the moss-covered wire, pinch the bunch together with your thumb and index finger. Hold this bunch together while preparing to secure everything with florist wire.

2: When using roses or larger statement flowers, you can keep them more secure and facing outward by creating a faux stem with florist wire. To do this, first cut off the stem of the rose, leaving about ½ inch from the base of the bloom.

3: Next, take a straight piece of florist wire and thread it through the stem and bloom, allowing the wire to go completely through the rose.

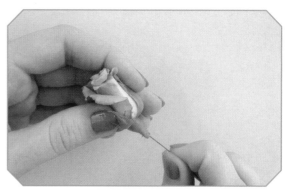

4: Create a small hook with the end of the florist wire that is closest to the bloom and pull it into the center of the rose to secure.

5: Use the faux rose stem you just created to wrap the rose into the growing strand of flowers, wrapping the florist wire stem around the moss-covered wire in a downward spiral motion.

6: Using the color and size pattern of your choice, continue adding groups of sprigs (2–4 each time) and roses to the growing strand to build your crown. Secure each new group into the strand with florist wire.

7: Your growing strand should look like this, with all the flowers facing the same side.

8: Once you have reached the desired crown length, take the end of the moss-covered florist wire and create a loop at the end of the strand.

9: Cut 2 pieces of ribbon, 1 yard each. Fold each piece in half and feed one through each loop, pulling through to create a loop knot on both sides. The ribbons will allow you to adjust the crown to fit on your head.

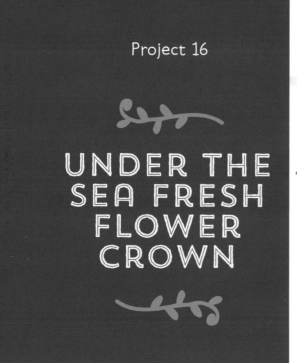

UNDER THE SEA FRESH FLOWER CROWN

Complete with shells and pearls, this flower crown is perfect for channeling your inner mermaid, costume party or not.

WHAT YOU WILL NEED

silver brunia, seeded eucalyptus, magenta celotias, purple scabiosas, light pink globe amaranth

assorted shells with holes

faux pearls with holes

small starfish

6–10 feet of florist wire

a 20- to 24-inch strand of moss-covered wire

scissors or garden shears

2 yards of ribbon

1: Begin by clipping and pinching 3–5 flower stems together (about 3 inches each) with your thumb and index finger. Place the small bunch about 2 inches away from the end of the moss-covered wire strand, preparing to secure everything together with florist wire.

2: With a 10- to 12-inch piece of florist wire, wrap the first group of flowers and moss-covered wire strand together, moving in a spiral motion from left to right. Add in a second bunch of flowers and repeat, wrapping the new group into the growing strand.

3: For a whimsical look, add shells by threading florist wire through their holes and securing to the crown by wrapping them into the growing flower chain.

TIP: To cover up the visible holes in the shells, weave in seeded Eecalyptus each time you add a shell. It organically masks the hole and can look like seaweed.

4: Add a small starfish and secure it to the growing strand with florist wire by wrapping the wire around and across the arms of the star.

5: Add pearls by threading the florist wire through them and wrapping each into the growing strand.

TIP: Inexpensive pearls can be purchased on stretchy bracelets at craft and accessory stores. Just clip the stretchy band and restring the pearls using florist wire to incorporate them into your crown.

6: Repeat step 3 when adding additional shells.

7: Continue to build the crown by adding in small bunches of flowers, shells, and pearls in a pattern of your choice.

8: Once you have reached the desired crown length, create a loop at each end of the moss-covered wire strand.

9: Wrap the end of the moss-covered wire loop in a spiral, beginning at the base of the loop and moving backward toward the flowers to cover any loose wire. This step helps to create a cleaner look at the ends of your crown and also creates a loop for threading ribbon.

10: Cut 2 pieces of ribbon, 1 yard each. Fold each piece in half and feed one through the loop on each side of the crown, creating a knot. The ribbons will allow you to adjust the crown to fit on your head.

Project 17

GREEK GODDESS FAUX IVY CROWN

This gold Grecian crown is great for costume parties and a quick alternative to an expensive Halloween accessory.

WHAT YOU WILL NEED

gold spray paint

scissors

1–2 feet of florist tape

a 20- to 24-inch strand of gold wire

approximately 3 feet of either faux or real ivy

1: Cover two 8-inch pieces of real or faux ivy in gold spray paint.

2: This is what your ivy should look like once covered.

3: Bend the strand of gold wire into a circle that fits around your head and twist the ends together to secure.

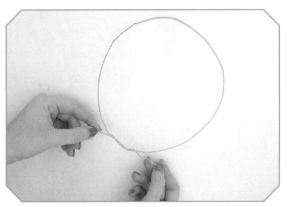

4: Prepare to attach one end of the first piece of ivy to the wire circle, making sure to identify the back and front of the wire circle (back is where the ends are twisted together, which will be covered with the ivy).

5: Attach the first piece of ivy to the circle using florist tape, wrapping the two together in three places to secure.

6: Layer a second piece of ivy over the first and prepare to attach it to the wire circle.

8: To cover the green florist tape, you can spray paint over the entire crown once more to make everything appear gold.

7: Attach the second piece of ivy to the circle, taping it to the wire in three places to secure.

WINTER

Brighten up cold winter days with these flower crowns and hairpieces designed to bring cheer even during the gloomiest days of the year. Holiday season is a great time to embrace berries or faux blooms when creating floral hair accessories.

HOLIDAY FRESH FLOWER CROWN

Wearing flowers in your hair is no longer just a summertime activity. Wear this fresh holiday flower crown during the holiday season (or anytime!) with a great red lip to create an instant outfit. Flowers used to create this crown include hypericum berries (in two different shades of red), freesia stems (any greenery will do!), and wax flower stems.

TIP: The wax flower stems have a great minty smell. Rosemary is also a great greenery replacement or addition to this flower crown because of its scent.

WHAT YOU WILL NEED

3–5 assorted seasonal flowers or berries of your choice

4–6 feet of florist wire

scissors or garden shears

2 yards of ribbon

1: Gather 3–5 stems of the hypericum berries and 1–2 sprigs of greenery, pinching all of the stems together with your index finger and thumb.

2: Begin wrapping the gathered group of stems together with a 10- to 12-inch piece of florist wire.

3: Wrap the florist wire around the bunch two to three times, moving the wire in a spiral motion from left to right.

4: Continue adding small bunches (2–4 stems each time) of assorted berries and greenery, creating a pattern of your choice with the flowers.

5: Wrap florist wire around the growing strand one to two times to secure each new bunch added.

6: Continue adding in small bunches of flowers and securing each to the growing strand with florist wire until you reach the desired length of your crown.

8: After pulling the slip knot tightly, use the two ends to tie a second knot to secure. Repeat on other side.

7: Cut the ribbon into two 1-yard pieces, one for each side of the finished flower crown. Fold each 1-yard piece in half, creating a loop, and secure one ribbon to each side of the gathered stems with a loop knot.

Project 19

FRESH FLOWER CROWN FROM THE GARDEN

The ingredients in this crown are not only great for cooking but also smell fresh and amazing when woven together. Here's a new reason to play with your food…

WHAT YOU WILL NEED

a variety of 3–5 herb garden staples such as mint rosemary lavender and brassica (e.g., kale)

4–6 feet of florist wire

a 20- to 24-inch strand of moss-covered wire

scissors or garden shears

2 yards of ribbon

1: Create the base of your flower crown using a piece of fresh rosemary approximately 3–4 inches long.

2: Wrap the rosemary to the moss-covered wire strand with florist wire, moving in a downward spiral motion.

3: Add a pinch of lavender and mint and prepare to twist them in with the rosemary and moss-covered wire using a new piece of florist wire.

4: Continue building the crown by placing a piece of the brassica at the end of the growing strand and using the florist wire to wrap it to the moss-covered wire strand.

5: Add a second piece of rosemary and mint once you have reached the end of the first and prepare to add it to the growing flower chain.

6: Continue wrapping in pieces of mint, lavender, brassica, and rosemary to the moss-covered wire with florist wire in the pattern of your choice.

7: Once you have reached your ideal crown length, finish the end of the strand by adding a final piece of rosemary and wrapping it to the moss-covered wire.

8: Once the rosemary is attached, clip away any excess wire.

9: Prepare to secure the two ends of the crown together by crossing the two moss-covered wire ends.

10: Wrap the ends together in a spiral motion to secure and finish the back of the flower crown.

Project 20

LA DOLCE VITA FAUX FLOWER HAIR CLIP

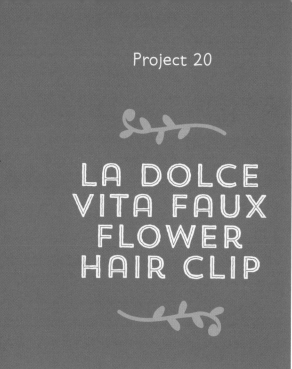

Accessorize your holiday outfits with this red rose hair clip that can quickly spice up any ponytail or bun. This piece can also be secured to a headband and worn with shorter hair.

WHAT YOU WILL NEED

one claw hair clip with holes at the top

scissors

2–4 feet of florist tape

4–6 faux red roses

a 14-to 16-inch strand of moss-covered wire

6–10 feet of florist wire

1: Begin by separating the faux roses from their stems.

2: Create wire stems for each of your roses. Depending on the types of faux roses you chose, this can be done in a couple of different ways. Option 1: If you chose a rose with a hole through the center, you should feed a 6- to 10-inch piece of florist wire through the center of the bloom and place the flower in the middle of the wire. Then, create a hook, bending the end of the wire back to meet the other end while placing it between the petals to hide the wire.

3: Pinch the two ends of wire together and twist tightly to form a pliable wire stem for the bloom.

4: Option 2: If you chose roses without holes through the center, you can begin creating the wire stem by pulling back a couple of the petals. Then, place the center of a 6- to 10-inch piece of wire where the petals meet the base of the bloom, hiding it inside of the rose. Make sure that the center of the wire is placed underneath the petals, as you will need the two ends of the wire to be at least 2–3 inches each.

5: Pull the ends of the wire behind the base of the rose and pinch them together.

6: Twist the two ends of wire together tightly to create the wire stem. If the rose does not feel secure on its new stem, repeat step 4 and move the wire through the petals on the opposite side of the flower, placing a second piece of wire under two different petals.

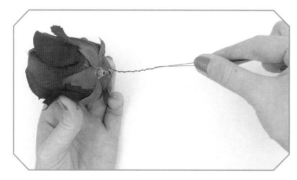

7: Once all of your roses are on new wire stems, you are ready to begin forming your design.

8: Begin creating your hair clip by placing one of the roses against the moss-covered wire, about ⅓ of the way from the end.

9: Bend the wire stem up to the right, preparing to wrap it around the moss-covered wire several times, moving from left to right.

10: Once the wire stem is completely wrapped around the moss-covered wire, add a second rose next to the first.

11: Repeat step 9 with the second rose.

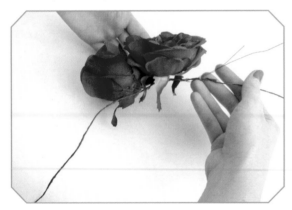

12: Continue placing your roses on the moss-covered wire strand and wrapping them in. The pliable wire stems will allow you to bend the roses into the design you want. For this project, I created a bit of a circle shape with the flowers rather than placing them in a straight line.

13: Once you have added all of your roses, prepare to cover the bottom of your design with florist tape. This will cover up any sharp wires and reinforce the flowers to the moss-covered wire base. The florist wire is tacky and will stick to itself. Just wrap it around the base in a circular motion until all of the wires are covered.

14: Once the base of your design is completely covered in florist tape, introduce the claw clip and prepare to attach it to the flowers.

15: Begin attaching the claw clip to your design by threading the end of the moss-covered wire through the hole in the clip on one side.

16: Bring the clip toward the group of flowers and pull tightly before wrapping the moss-covered wire around the hole in the clip. Make sure to wrap the moss-covered wire around the clip approximately four to six times to secure. Repeat this step on the opposite side, wrapping the other end of the moss-covered wire around the other side of the clip to finish.

SPECIAL OCCASIONS

From birthdays to baby showers, flower crowns are the perfect accessory or gift for the guest of honor on her special day.

BIRTHDAY FRESH FLOWER CROWN

This bright and colorful fresh flower crown is perfect for a birthday celebration—or any celebration!

WHAT YOU WILL NEED

8–12 fresh flowers (I used ranunculus, but spray roses, daisies, mums, and many other seasonal varieties are great replacements)

6–8 feet of florist wire

20–24 inches of moss-covered wire

scissors or garden shears

2 yards of ribbon

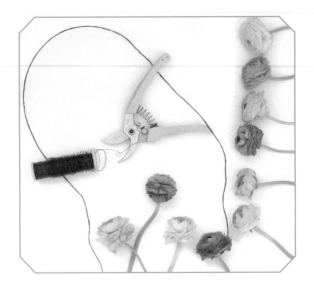

1: Cut off the stem of each ranunculus bloom about ¼ inch away from the flower.

2: Cut one 4-inch piece of florist wire for each ranunculus bloom.

3: Feed a 4-inch piece of florist wire through the center of the remaining stem and completely through the flower.

4: Create a small hook with the end of the florist wire and carefully pull it into the bloom, securing the wire to the center of the flower without ripping through it.

5: Repeat steps 3 and 4 for each flower you plan to incorporate into the crown, ultimately creating new wire stems for each of the flowers.

7: Repeat step 6 for each bloom, placing them about 1 inch apart (the distance between each flower will depend on the size of the bloom). The moss-covered wire will serve as the base for your crown with each bloom secured to it with florist wire.

6: Place the bottom of the ranunculus bloom against the moss-covered wire and bend its wire stem up to the right. Wrap the florist wire from the bottom of the bloom around the moss-covered wire several times, moving in a spiral motion from left to right.

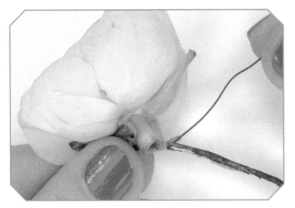

TIP: This is what the bottom of your crown should begin to look like as you add in each bloom.

8: Continue adding in ranunculus until you have reached the desired crown length.

9: Create a loop with the end of the moss-covered wire and cut off the excess. Repeat on other side.

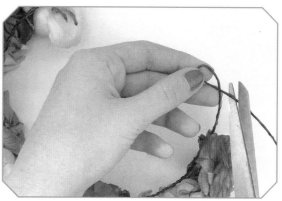

10: Wrap the excess of the moss-covered wire around the ends of the stems to secure, ultimately creating a loop at each end of the crown that ribbon can be strung through. If you choose not to use ribbon, these loops also provide a great base for securing the crown to the head with bobby pins or hair clips.

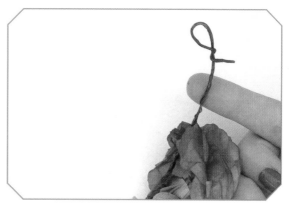

BABY SHOWER FRESH FLOWER CROWN: IT'S A BOY!

Welcome a new baby boy with this fresh blue flower crown made of cheerful delphiniums. Blue hydrangeas are also a great option!

WHAT YOU WILL NEED

seasonal flowers of your choice

scissors or garden shears

4–6 feet of florist wire

20–24 inches of moss-covered wire

1: Begin by clipping the delphinium flowers from the bunch, leaving about 3 inches of stem on each.

2: Lay out all of your clipped pieces for easy access. For this crown, you may use anywhere from 20–40 blooms depending on how long or full you want the finished piece to be.

3: Place one of your clipped flowers against the moss-covered wire starting about 3 inches from the end.

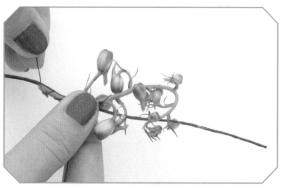

4: Secure the clipped bloom to the moss-covered wire by pinching the two together with your thumb and index finger and wrapping them with florist wire two to three times in a spiral motion, moving from left to right.

5: Continue building a growing chain of flowers while using the moss-covered wire as a base. Add one to three blooms at a time, wrapping the florist wire around each group of stems to secure.

TIP: For more delicate stems, be careful not to wrap too tightly or they may tear.

6: As you secure each group of stems to the moss-covered wire, create a growing chain of flowers that looks like this from the bottom side.

7: Once you have reached the desired flower crown length, cut off the excess moss-covered wire, leaving enough length on either side to completely wrap the finished piece around the head.

8: Twist the ends of the moss-covered wire together to create a complete circle to finish the crown.

BABY SHOWER FRESH FLOWER CROWN: IT'S A GIRL!

Welcome a new baby girl with this pretty-in-pink design.

WHAT YOU WILL NEED

20–25 small to medium pink blooms such as spray roses (include leaves if desired)

4–6 feet of florist wire

a 20- to 24-inch strand of moss-covered wire

scissors or garden shears

2 yards of ribbon

1: Begin by placing one spray rose and leaf approximately 2–3 inches away from the end of the moss-covered wire strand, preparing to secure everything together with a piece of florist wire.

2: Wrap the stem of the first rose and leaf to the moss-covered wire with a 10- to 12-inch piece of florist wire, moving from left to right in a spiral motion. Add a second rose and repeat.

3: Continue building a flower chain by adding one rose at a time and periodically incorporating a leaf. This is what the back of your crown should look like.

4: Once you have reached your desired crown length, secure the flower chain with the end of the florist wire, clipping off any excess.

5: Create a loop with the end of the moss-covered wire.

6: Wrap the end of the moss-covered wire loop in a spiral, moving backward toward the flowers and covering any loose florist wire. This step creates a cleaner look at the ends of your crown and also creates a loop for threading ribbon.

7: Cut 2 pieces of ribbon, 1 yard each. Fold each piece in half, creating a loop, and feed one through each side of the moss-covered wire circle.

8: Pull the ends of the ribbon through the loop, creating a knot to secure each end.

BOHO BRIDE FRESH FLOWER HAIRPIECE

This simple floral hairpiece looks amazing pinned into an updo and can be either subdued or over-the-top, depending on the colors and types of flowers you choose to incorporate. For this particular project, I used a rare and special fresh flower appropriately called "Blushing Bride," along with light pink globe amaranth for additional texture. To create your own custom look, substitute these with seasonal blooms of your choice.

TIP: This project can also double as a boutonniere!

WHAT YOU WILL NEED

2–4 assorted flowers of your choice

1–2 feet of florist wire

1 foot of florist tape

scissors

4–6 bobby pins to secure the finished piece into the hair

1: Snip the stems of each flower at about 2–3 inches from the base of the bloom.

2: Gather and pinch 3 larger blooms together with your thumb and index finger.

3: Continue to add in the flowers of your choice, styling them into a bundle and pinching all stems together at the base of the stems

TIP: To create a more bohemian look, place the flowers into the bundle at varying heights for a perfectly imperfect look.

4: Wrap florist wire tightly around the base of the gathered bundle approximately five to six times.

5: Cut the stems about 1½ inches away from the base of the bundle of blooms, making them all the same length.

6: Cut 1 foot of florist tape and prepare to wrap the gathered stems together.

7: Wrap all of the stems together with the florist tape, moving from the base of the bloom down to the ends of the stems in a spiral motion to cover the entire bundle. The florist tape is very tacky and will adhere to itself and the stems very easily.

8: Once you have covered the stems with florist tape, cut off any excess tape. Use bobby pins to secure the finished piece into the hair.

TIP: You can also secure this piece on a lapel with straight pins if you choose to use it as a boutonniere.

BRIDESMAID FRESH FLOWER CROWN

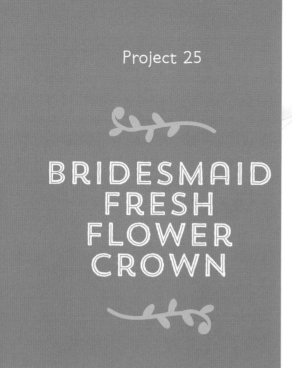

These colorful flower crowns are great for bridesmaids, no matter what hairstyle they choose. This look is simple enough to be worn alongside a crown braid, with an updo, or paired with flowing locks. The flowers used to create this crown include (left to right) pink wax flowers, small pink bouvardia flowers, and pink limonium.

WHAT YOU WILL NEED

a variety of 3–5 small flowers

4–6 feet of florist wire

20–24 inches of moss-covered wire

scissors or garden shears

2 yards of ribbon

1: Begin by clipping 2–4 sprigs (about 2½–3 inches each) of one small flower and pinching the bunch together with your thumb and index finger. Then, secure the bunch of flowers to the moss-covered wire by wrapping a 10- to 12-inch piece of florist wire around the bundle two to three times. Leave about 2–3 inches at one end of the moss-covered wire.

2: Continue clipping and pinching small groups of flowers together in the order of your choice and preparing to add them to the growing chain.

3: Carefully secure each group of flowers to the moss-covered wire by continuously wrapping the florist wire around the bundle in a spiral motion. Wrap the florist wire only one to two times around for each group of flowers added.

4: Continue steps 2 and 3 while creating a pattern of your choice using small groups of flowers. Repeat this step until you have reached the desired length of your flower crown.

5: Once you have reached the desired length, cut the remaining stems the same length, leaving the moss-covered wire intact.

6: Create a loop with the excess moss-covered wire on both sides of the finished crown.

7: Wrap the excess moss-covered wire around the base of the loop, covering the ends of the stems.

8: Cut the ribbon into two 1-yard pieces, one for each side of the finished flower crown. Fold each 1-yard piece in half and feed one through each moss-covered wire loop before securing with a loop knot.

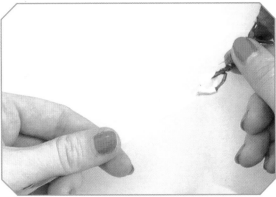

BRIDAL SHOWER FRESH FLOWER CROWN

Perfect for a bride-to-be, this fresh crown made of white freesias, small white phlox flowers, and greenery smells as sweet as it looks.

WHAT YOU WILL NEED

assorted white and green flowers

4–6 feet of florist wire

scissors or garden shears

2 yards of ribbon

1: Begin by clipping and pinching 3–5 flower stems together (about 3 inches each) with your thumb and index finger, preparing to wrap them together with florist wire.

2: Begin forming a flower chain by wrapping small groups of flowers together with florist wire in a spiral motion from left to right. Wrap each new piece one to two times to the growing chain.

TIP: Place each group of flowers close together for a larger, fuller crown. You can also create a sparser and smaller crown by spreading the groups of flowers out and adding fewer blooms at a time.

3: Repeat steps 1 and 2 until you have reached your desired crown length.

TIP: Alternate larger and smaller blooms for a more balanced look. Placing all of the larger blooms to one side of the crown can also create an asymmetrical look.

4: Once your crown is as long as you want it to be, securely wrap the remaining stems four to five times with florist wire to secure.

5: To ensure that your finished crown is balanced on both sides, pinch a final bundle together that reflects that of the first piece you used. Make sure that this bundle is facing the opposite way on the crown from the other pieces you have added.

6: Secure the new bundle to the finished strand with a 10- to 12-inch piece of florist wire, wrapping all of the stems together about four to six times.

8: Once the first knot is complete, gather the ends of the ribbon and tie them together into a second and final knot for security. Repeat on the opposite side.

7: Cut the ribbon into two 1-yard pieces, one for each side of the finished flower crown. Then, fold 1 yard of ribbon in half and tie a loop knot around the end of the crown, leaving at least half an inch from the edge of the stems.

FAUX GARDENIA HAIR COMB

This faux gardenia hair comb is easy to wear with updos or ponytails and adds an element of simple sophistication to any bridal or formal look. Fresh blooms can also be used for this project.

WHAT YOU WILL NEED

1 faux gardenia bloom (faux dahlias or peonies also work well)

1–2 feet of florist wire

1 large hair comb

12–14 inches of florist tape

scissors

1: Remove the gardenia bloom from its faux stem.

2: Create a pliable wire stem for the gardenia by pulling two of the petals back and placing the center of a 12- to 14-inch piece of florist wire against the base of the flower petal.

3: Bring the two ends of florist wire together at the base of the original stem and pull tightly from the center of the flower, allowing the wire to hold the bloom together where the base of the petals meet the stem.

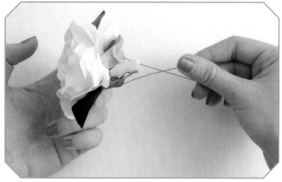

4: Twist the two ends of the florist wire together tightly, creating a faux stem that holds the bloom in place.

5: Introduce the comb and place the top of it at the base of the gardenia bloom where the new wire stem has replaced the original.

6: Use the new wire stem to tightly secure the gardenia to the hairpiece by threading it through the comb sporadically around the base.

7: To prevent the wire from pulling hair or scratching the head, cover it with a layer of florist tape, using the same motion as in step 6.

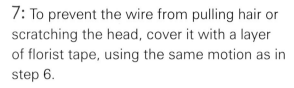

8: Completely cover the wire with florist tape for a second layer of security to finish the hairpiece.

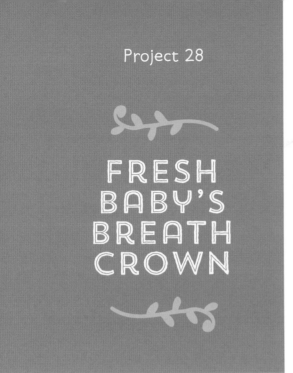

FRESH BABY'S BREATH CROWN

Perfect for a flower girl and made with simple baby's breath, this sweet flower crown is easy and inexpensive to create. Baby's breath may have a bad reputation when placed in a flower arrangement, but it looks delicate in a flower crown and is always in season.

WHAT YOU WILL NEED

1 bundle of baby's breath (about 3–5 larger stems)

6–8 feet of florist wire

18- to 20-inch strand of moss-covered wire

scissors or garden shears

2 yards of ribbon

1: Clip small sprigs of baby's breath from the larger stems into 2- to 4-inch pieces.

2: Gather 2–3 sprigs and pinch them together with your thumb and index finger. Place the small bundle about 2–3 inches from the end of the moss-covered wire strand and prepare to secure everything together with florist wire.

3: Begin securing the baby's breath bundle to the moss-covered wire by wrapping the two together with florist wire, moving in a spiral clockwise motion.

4: Continue adding small groups of baby's breath and wrapping them to the growing strand.

TIP: For a fuller, larger crown, add larger bundles of baby's breath and wrap them tightly together. For a thinner, sparser crown, add smaller bundles and wrap them farther apart.

5: Repeat step 4 until you have reached the desired crown length.

6: Create a loop with the end of the moss-covered wire and wrap the end of the strand in a spiral, beginning at the base of the loop moving backward toward the flowers to cover any loose florist wire. Repeat on the other side.

7: Cut 2 pieces of ribbon, 1 yard each. Fold each piece in half and feed one through each of the two loops you just created.

8: Pull the ends of the ribbon through the loop and secure with a knot. Repeat on the other side. The ribbons will allow you to adjust the crown to fit on the head.

WHIMSICAL FRESH FLOWER CROWN

Perfect for the whimsical bride, this flower crown made with textured flowers and greenery is formed into two layers for added volume.

WHAT YOU WILL NEED

greenery such as rose leaves and seeded eucalyptus

white medium-sized blooms such as ranunculus

scissors and garden shears

a 30- to 35-inch strand of grapevine

4–6 feet of florist wire

1: Gather 2–3 small sprigs of greenery, cutting and the stems so they are no longer than 3–4 inches. Along with the grapevine, pinch the bunch together with your thumb and index finger. Begin forming your crown by wrapping florist wire around this bunch to secure.

2: Add one of your white flowers to the base of the greenery, covering the wrapped wire with the bloom and preparing to wrap it into the growing strand.

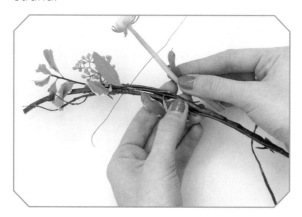

3: Secure the white flower to the bundle with florist wire by wrapping them together in a downward spiral motion two to three times around.

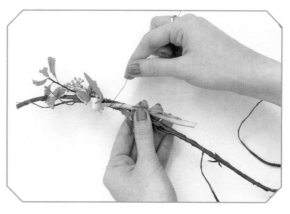

4: Add more greenery and secure it to the bundle by wrapping the stem to the growing strand with florist wire.

5: Continue adding the white flowers in one by one and wrapping them to the bundle in a pattern of your choice.

6: Once you have created a floral chain that is approximately 28–30 inches long, pull one end toward the center of the strand to form a circle.

7: Secure the end to the middle of the chain by wrapping the two together with a new piece of florist wire, covering the wire with greenery where possible.

8: Prepare to connect the other end of the chain to the circle to form a double layer.

9: Connect the second end of the chain to the other side of the circle, allowing the second layer to sit on top of the first for added volume.

10: Once both ends are connected to the circle, the finished crown should look like this.

ROMANTIC FRESH FLOWER CROWN

This feminine and romantic flower crown is made with beautiful pink garden roses, dahlias, ranunculus, and greenery. The focal point of this crown is intentionally placed at the back of the head, adding an element of surprise and romanticism.

WHAT YOU WILL NEED

greenery such as seeded eucalyptus or leaves

statement blooms like garden roses, dahlias, and ranunculus

garden shears or scissors

a 20- to 24-inch strand of moss-covered wire

4–6 feet of florist wire

1: Cut a 4- to 6-inch stem of greenery and prepare to attach it to the moss-covered wire strand with a 6- to 10-inch piece of florist wire.

2: Secure the greenery to one end of the moss-covered wire by wrapping the two together with florist wire, moving from left to right. Leave approximately 3–4 inches of moss-covered wire at one end.

3: Add 1–2 more sprigs of greenery to the bundle, wrapping everything together with florist wire from left to right to create a growing floral chain.

4: Once you have woven approximately 4–6 inches of greenery into the growing chain, begin adding your statement flowers. Secure each to the growing chain with florist wire by wrapping them to the bundle in a spiral motion from left to right.

5: Continue adding your statement flowers one by one in the pattern of your choice. Wrap each to the growing floral chain with florist wire.

7: Finish the floral chain by adding greenery on the opposite side (repeating steps 1–3) and pulling the two ends together.

6: After adding the statement flowers, continue filling out the middle of the crown with fuller pieces such as the seeded eucalyptus.

8: Twist the two ends of moss-covered wire to form the finished crown.

SUPPLY RESOURCES AND RECOMMENDATIONS

A.C. Moore Arts and Crafts
www.acmoore.com

Afloral.com
www.afloral.com

Beverly Fabrics
www.beverlys.com

Dutch Flower Line
beta.dutchflowerline.com

Jamali Floral and Garden Supplies
www.jamaligarden.com

Jo-Ann Fabric and Craft Store
www.joann.com

JRose Wholesale Flowers
www.jrosewholesaleflowers.com

Michaels Arts & Crafts
www.michaels.com

PANY Floral Corporation
PANYSilk.com

For fresh flowers, shop from your local flower market, grocery store, or deli.

ACKNOWLEDGMENTS

Thank you to my friends and family for all of your support while creating this book. Luke, I could not have done this without you. Joanna, Jessica, Dayna, Lindsay, and Treasure, thank you for always allowing me to take photos of your beautiful faces in my flower crowns. Your love and support has meant so much to me throughout this process.

ABOUT THE AUTHOR

Christy Meisner Doramus is a New York–based flower hair accessory designer with Southern roots. While growing up in Louisiana, she and her mother designed dresses and accessories together, an interest that has been a major part of her life. Christy attended the Art Institute of California in San Francisco. There, she studied fashion marketing and management and went on to become a beauty publicist in Manhattan. Christy's love for design, creativity, and fresh flowers led her to begin CrownsbyChristy.com, her own custom flower crown company. She currently lives in Manhattan with her husband, Luke, who receives most of the photography credits for this book.

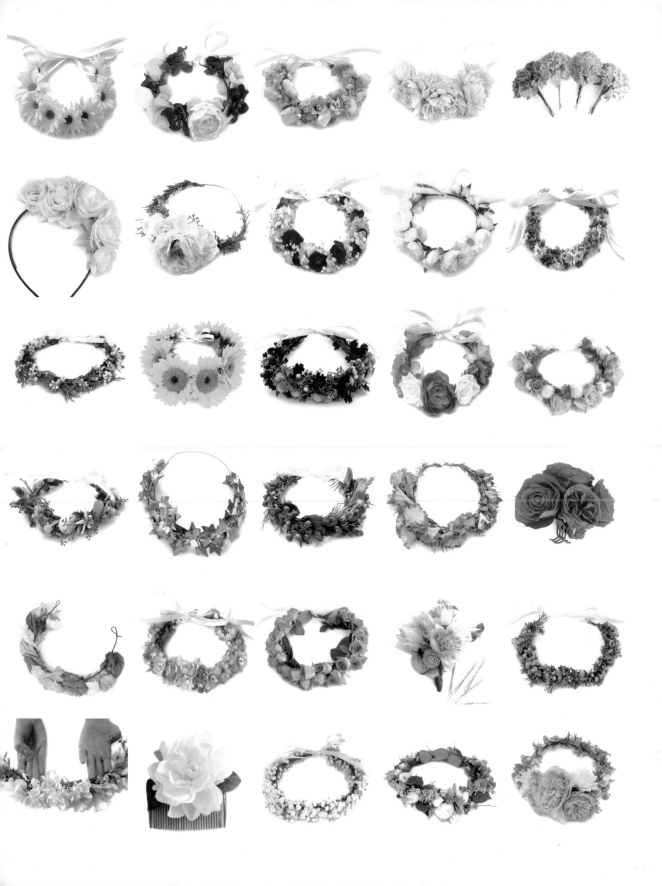